Growing Your Ministry God's Way

(Using Your Spiritual Gifts)

Gertrude Joanne Pollard-Watts

ISBN 978-0-578-46508-1 (paperback)

Copyright © 2019 by Gertrude Joanne Pollard-Watts

All rights reserved. No part of this publication may be reproduced, distributed, or transmitted in any form or by any means, including photocopying, recording, or other electronic or mechanical methods without the prior written permission of the publisher. For permission requests, solicit the publisher via the email address below.

Gertrude Joanne Pollard- Watts
5036 Hardy McManus Road
Evans, Georgia 30809
Email: gjpwatts.teach@gmail.com

Printed in the United States of America

Note: All Bible verses symbolize *"Key Principles"*

Contents

Thank You, God 7

Dedication 9

Introduction..11

Why God Gives Spiritual Gifts..13

Recognizing Your Spiritual Gift/s 14

Understanding What Spiritual Gift/s Entail 16

How to Use Your Spiritual Gift/s God's Way and Reap
    a Harvest in Your Ministry 25

How to Sustain Your Ministry...29

A Blessed Ministry Brings Forth Growth in the Church 31

Thanking God in All Things..32

Conclusion...35

About the Author..37

Thank You, God

Thank you, God, for the love, mercy, grace, protection, and favor you are giving me throughout life. I thank you for accepting me into your family in Christ Jesus and using me for your glory. Thank you for continuing to guide me with your words, instructions, wisdom, knowledge, and understanding and giving me the strength and obedience in following you, Jesus. I recognize sometimes I fell short, but you allow me to repent and get back on the right track. Thank you, my Heavenly Father, for supplying all my needs according to your riches and glory and allowing me to write this book by the guidance of your Holy Spirit as well as the anointing of your words to manifest in the lives and ministries of the readers. And thank you, God, for continuing to reveal to me your destiny for my life, as scripture says in Jeremiah 29:11 (NIV), "For I know the plans I have for you, declares the LORD, plans to prosper you and not to harm you, plans to give you hope and a future."

Dedication

Thank you, God, for a praying mother in Christ. I dedicate this book to my dear mother, Josephine Pollard Mason, 82, who has been there for me through all the trials and tribulations in my life, praying along the way for me. Her unfailing love never stops flowing, and her sacrifices—though many—allowed me to become the person I am today. Her helping hands never stopped helping no matter what bridges I had to cross. Her listening ears never stopped listening whether there was good or bad news. She always pointed me toward Christ. My dear mother is certainly a strong pillar in my life who is anchored in Jesus Christ.

Next, I dedicate this book to my daughter, Gabriele Pollard Watts, also known as "Gabbie," who was brought up in a Christian home and from a young age watched her mother grow in the love of Jesus Christ. She always enlightens me with encouraging words and the phrase, "I love you Mommy," in every conversation.

Also, this book is dedicated to my goddaughter, Stacy Faison, who has grown up to be a beautiful young lady who has taught me so much in life by her actions. She has always shown me the love of Jesus by her warm smiles and laughs, which let me know that everything is okay.

This book is also dedicated to Jasmine Dawson and Maria Bennett, whom I call my daughters and who always greet me with big smiles and warm hugs. I appreciate their willingness to help me when needed.

Next, this book is dedicated to my dear friends/sisters in Christ—Charlene B. Sledge, who inspires me and gives me words of encouragement when we are walking/ jogging around the track; Angela Snell, who is a great listener and listens to me and suggests solutions; and Constance Ceasar, who provides spiritual support when needed and a bunch of laughs that connects me to my inner peace. I thank God for my close friends who have been my inspirational support and whom I can always go to when needed, and I dedicate this book to my family and loved ones who gave me words of kindness and prayed for me. Christians all over are looking for ways to grow their ministries God's way, and this book is also dedicated to them.

Introduction

There have been numerous occasions where the church of God has been in a suffering state when it comes to having a thriving ministry. It seems like no matter what techniques are being used, the decaying effects are still noticed within the ministry and also being seen by others outside of the ministry. Christians may ask questions such as: why is this happening? Am I in the right ministry? Why is my ministry falling apart? Why is my ministry not bringing forth disciples? Well, many Christians are asking the same questions, and this book will shine some light on how God has provided principles for his children to use along with their spiritual gifts. It doesn't matter what spiritual gift/s you may have been blessed with or what ministry you are called to serve; these principles will work in each one. Our Heavenly Father has provided everything we need to know in his Word that will change all circumstances that go against his kingdom building. All ministries of God are for the edification of His name and for the building of His kingdom. One of the principles that will be talked about in this book is the principle of love. Having a loving spirit is the foundation of a successful ministry. Also, spiritual gifts are key elements in growing your ministry and will be discussed in detail. So if you truly want to grow your ministry God's way, this book is what you need to read and then apply the principles into your ministry in order for it to become successful. You will be able to reach your God-given potential in your ministry. Before you get started reading the chapters, I have one request—that you pray and ask God to give you an open mind, clarity, and understanding of the principles that are given in this book so it will be used in "faith" to grow your ministry God's way.

Why God Gives Spiritual Gifts

*"God blesses his children to be
a blessing to others."*

There are many kinds of spiritual gifts God has given his children of believers to use for kingdom building. Sometimes we use them without knowing, and sometimes we know that we are spiritually gifted but are afraid to use them. My word to you is don't be afraid to use your spiritual gift/s because exercising your faith to use your gift/s for building up the kingdom of God is just what He wants us to do. God wants us to make a difference in the world in which we live by pointing people to Christ by our words and actions. It can be as simple as giving someone a smile when they are having a bad day or just saying thank you when someone opens a door for you. Just imagine if all the people in the world would use their spiritual gift/s in a positive way…many lives would be changed. Senseless ungodly acts of all kinds would be eliminated. We would meet happier, caring, loving, selfless people in the world. But even though this may seem a little farfetched in this day and time, we know that when Jesus Christ returns, the kingdom of God will reign (1 Corinthians 15:24). But just because we know that doesn't mean we should not use our spiritual gifts. So let's get started now and help make this world a better place by touching the lives of others through sharing the hope and love of Jesus Christ.

Recognizing Your Spiritual Gift/s

"True ministry is exercising the principles of God with your spiritual gifts."

What are spiritual gifts and why do we need them? God has given everyone spiritual gifts in order to edify his name and also for the building up of His kingdom. Spiritual gifts are blessings that come from the Lord and are used for His glory. When they're used in the proper way, not only will they be a blessing to others, but the Church will also become the church God wants it to be. Even though there are many different kinds of spiritual gifts, all comes from the same spirit, and that is the Spirit of the Lord. In Romans 12:6–8 (NIV), one will find some of the gifts of the Spirit. Many of God's people have been blessed with them. They are essential to the growth of the body of the church and its ministries. These spiritual gifts are: "the gift of prophesy, serving, teaching, encouraging, contributing to the needs of others, leadership, and showing mercy." Other spiritual gifts are found in 1 Corinthians 12:7–11, "which speaks of gifts such as: the gift of wisdom, knowledge, faith, healing, miraculous powers, prophecy, discerning between spirits, speaking in tongues, and another's who are gifted with the interpretation of tongues." In Ephesians 4:11, "God also gives some to be apostles, prophets, evangelists, pastors, and teachers." No matter what your spiritual gifts may be, "they are all given to prepare God's people for works of service so that the body of Christ may be built up until we all reach unity in the faith and the knowledge of the Son of God and become mature, attaining to the whole measure of the fullness of Christ."

Understanding What Spiritual Gift/s Entail

"Understanding opens the doors to growth."

God has blessed his children when he made them in his image. In the divine Word, it states "So, God created man in his own image, in the image of God he created him; male and female he created them" (Genesis 1:27). So when you are using your spiritual gift/s, you are using what God has given you in his likeness and for his glory. Don't let your spiritual gift/s be unused before you exit this earth. Glorify God to the highest! Understanding what spiritual gifts entail is very important. They are given for a purpose, and that purpose is through the Word of God, bringing forth hope, love, unity, and disciples through the ministries of God (1 Peter 4:10-11) states, "Each one should use whatever gift he or she has received to serve others, faithfully administering God's grace in its various forms. If anyone speaks, he should do it as one speaking the very words of God. If anyone serves, he should do it with the strength God provides, so that in all things God may be praised through Jesus Christ. To him be the glory and the power for ever and ever. Amen. Each person of God has the ability to do so when using their Spiritual gift/s God's way."

When it comes to the *spiritual gift of prophecy*, many are not using this gift in the modern-day world. It is looked down upon and is usually quenched by the gifted one. The gift of prophecy on one hand carries unwanted connotations in the eyes of some people, but on the other hand and in the eyes of the Lord, it is a gift that is much needed to uplift the body of the church when things such as encouragement, direction, correction, hope, love, and unity are needed in the body of Christ. Men and women must not speak from the human flesh, but while listening to the voice of God, allow the Holy Spirit to be their guide when using this gift (2 Peter 1:20–21). The church should also be aware of false prophets because there are many that exist in the world in which we live. The apostle John in 1 John 4:1–2 "tells us to test the spirit to see whether it is from God." This is how you recognize the Spirit of God, and every spirit that acknowledges that Jesus Christ has come in the flesh is from God, but every spirit that does not acknowledge Jesus is not from God."

Some of God's children are blessed with the wonderful *spiritual gift of serving*; they are the ones who want to serve others. In Matthew 20:28, it tells us that "just as the Son of Man did not come to be served, but to serve, and give his life as a ransom for many," the gift of serving can be carried out in many ways. Servers make sure the needs of others become their focus in their lives and work toward meeting the needs of the receiver. Knowing that they have met the needs of others pushes them to continue using their gift of serving for the building up of the kingdom of God. God has placed his servants all over the earth, and kingdom work is being done all over the world in modern time. In Matthew 25:35, Jesus said, "For I was hungry and you gave me something to eat, I was thirsty and you gave me something to drink, I was a stranger and you invited me in, I needed clothes and you clothed me, I was sick and you looked after me, I was in prison and you came to visit me." In Matthew 25:40, "The king replied, I tell you the truth, whatever you did for one of the least of these brothers of mine, you did for me." So use your gift of serving to glorify the Lord to the highest and bring blessing to the church, your community, and around the world.

Another *spiritual gift of preaching and teaching*. Preachers and teachers have a great responsibility of carrying the Word of God not only to his children but also to the world. The Word of God should be guided by the Holy Spirit as it unfolds into the lives of others while coming alive in their minds and actions. In 2 Timothy 4:2–5, it states, " Preach the Word; be prepared in season and out of season; correct, rebuke and encourage—with great patience and careful instruction. For the time will come when men will not put up with sound doctrine. Instead, to suit their own desires, they will gather around them a great number of teachers to say what their itching ears want to hear. They will turn their ears away from the truth and turn aside to myths. But you, keep your head in all situations, endure hardship, do the work of an evangelist, discharge all the duties of your ministry." Christians that deliver the Word correctly will point people to Christ, and Christians that carry it incorrectly will drive people away from our Heavenly Father or make their followers corrupted like the carrier. It states in Matthew 15:14, "Leave them; they are blind guides. If a blind man leads a blind man, both will fall into a pit."

The Word of God is very powerful. So spiritual preachers and teachers teach the divine Word of God from the most important book in the world—the Bible (Basic Instruction Before Leaving Earth)—which God has made available for our guidance. If this is your gift, remember the scripture in Titus 2:7–8, "In everything set them an example by doing what is good. In your teaching show integrity, seriousness and soundness of speech that cannot be condemned, so that those who oppose you may be ashamed because they have nothing bad to say about us." The *spiritual gift of encouragement* is a gift which everyone can benefit from, from time to time. It's a spiritual gift that uplifts the soul of a person and allows him/her to press on during life's toughest battles or to give encouragement to the church for the uplifting of the kingdom of the Lord during trying times. In Romans 12:8, it states, "If it is encouraging, let him encourage." It can also be referred to as the spirit of exhortation. So use this gift often to help grow your ministry.

The next spiritual gift that God has blessed some of his children with is the *spiritual gift of contributing*, where contributing can come in many forms. It can come in the form of giving up your time to help keep up the sanctuary, mowing an elderly person's lawn, cleaning the house of someone who has come home after being hospitalized, giving to the needs of children who don't have food on their tables or clothes on their backs, etc. Romans 12:8 states, "If it is contributing to the needs of others, let him give generously." When it comes to the *spiritual gift of leadership*, one should not take it lightly. The pastor/shepherd falls under this category, and Romans 12:8 states, "If it is leadership, let him govern diligently." Preachers must always remember that God is the center of church and govern accordingly. But Apostle Paul also gave a command to the followers in 1 Thessalonians 5:12–13, which states, "Now we ask you, brothers, to respect those who work hard among you, who are over you in the Lord and who admonish you. Hold them in highest regard in love because of their work. Live in peace with each other." God knew that his children were going to need instructions, so he sent the men/women of God (pastors, preachers, and teachers) to guide his children while on earth. His children need not only his teachings but also the mercy of God. It will come in one's ministry or in the community for whatever the reason it may be. God is expecting his Christian leaders and followers of his Son Jesus Christ to be merciful; therefore, Scripture tells us in Romans 12:8, "When showing mercy, let him do it cheerfully.

Some of God's children are ordinarily blessed with the *spiritual gift of showing mercy*. This brings to mind the parable in the

Bible of the king who took pity and canceled the debt of his servant and let him go (Matthew 18:23–27). This parable brings up another important principle, which comes from Matthew 7:12, which states, "So in everything, do to others what you would have them do to you, for this is sums up in the Law and the Prophets…" The parable continues in Matthew 18: 28–35, which narrates that the servant went out and found one of his fellow servants who owed him money; he became abusive to him and demanded him to pay back what he owed him (what a short memory he had!), and then the fellow servant fell to his knees and begged him to have mercy on him and to be patient with him because he will pay him back. But the servant refused and had the servant thrown into prison…But when the king who had pardoned the servant's debts heard about the actions of his servant, he called him in and brought to his memory how he showed mercy on him and canceled his account and that he should have shown the same mercy to his fellow servant. In anger, his master turned him over to the jailers to be tortured until he paid back all what he had owed. So another principle is stated in verse 35: "This is how our Heavenly Father will treat each of us unless we forgive our brother from the heart."

Let's look at another spiritual gift…Some of God's children are blessed with the *spiritual gift of wisdom*, for the Lord gives wisdom, and from his mouth come knowledge and understanding (Proverbs 2:6). Sometimes in life, unexpected circumstances will happen in our ministry, such as lack of participation, members showing up late or not showing up at all, sickness, problems in the home, etc., and that's why God gives his children wisdom so they can withstand the trials and tribulations in life as our faith in God takes us through. In the book of James 1:5, it states, "If any of you lacks wisdom, he should ask God, who gives generously to all without finding fault, and it will be given to him." Praise God! The *spiritual gift of knowledge* is also known as the "word of knowledge" and is related to the spiritual gift of wisdom. Knowledge is a gift of the Holy Spirit that enables one to bring understanding of things that are naturally understood by reason and are revealed to us by faith through the Holy Spirit, and only the Holy Spirit can reveal its divine knowledge. It says in 1 Corinthians 12:8, "To one there is given through the Spirit the message of wisdom, to another the message of knowledge by means of the same Spirit."

Another important gift God gives is the *spiritual gift of faith*, "true saving faith," God gives to his children. In Ephesians 2:8, it states, "For it is by grace you have been saved, through faith-and this not from yourselves, it is the gift of God- not by works, so that no one can boast." This gift of faith is the vessel by which we receive salvation from God. On the other hand, God gives to some the spiritual gift of faith (great faith), which displays a high confidence in God and his power and his promises to the point where their faith inspired them to do the will and trust in the Lord, no matter what the consequences may bring. The Roman centurion in Matthew 8:6-10 showed great faith when he asked Jesus to heal his paralyzed servant. In Hebrew 11:1 (KJV), it states, "Now faith is the substance of things hoped for, and the evidence of things not seen." Others who displayed great faith in the Bible are Noah, Abraham, Jacob, Daniel, Ester, Ruth, and David, just to name of few. God has also given some of his children great faith to be used in modern day to uplift the church and to encourage them to be of good cheer while doing the will of the Lord.

Another gift which God has given to some of his children is the *spiritual gift of healing*. During Jesus's ministry on earth, he went about healing the sick. His love and compassion for them inspired him to heal all sorts of ailments such as fever, being demon-possessed, leprosy, a paralysis, a shriveled hand, an issue of the blood, etc. (Mark. 1:29–34, 2:5, 3:1–5, 5:21–43; Luke 7:1–10). Even though God has blessed some of his children with the spiritual gift of healing, one must remember that it is God who is doing the healing through his children, if that is his divine will at that time. Sometimes we have seen in his Word that his disciples healed many, but there was a time even Jesus disciples were powerless and were not able to heal a possessed man (Matthew 14–20). Their so little faith prevented them from the divine healing. Nevertheless, this did not stop the disciples from believing in their spiritual gift of healing. They continued to show compassion and love for the sick as they trusted and had faith in God while praying and believing in his healing powers. God's children who are living in modern-day times and are blessed with the spiritual gift of healing must show the same kind of tenacity toward the sick as they use their spiritual gift of healing with compassion, love, and faith. The children of God must not forget the agony, pain and suffering our Heavenly Father allowed his Son Jesus Christ to go through for our healing. Isaiah 53:5 states "But he was pierced for our transgressions, he was crushed for our iniquities; the punishment that brought us peace was upon him, and by his wounds we are healed."

When it comes to being blessed with the *spiritual gift of miraculous powers*, also known as *"working of miracles,"* God gave his disciple the authority/power to cast out unclean spirits of all sorts (Mark 6:7; Acts 2:43). Some of God's children in this era in the church are blessed with this divine gift for the betterment of the church and glorifying the Lord. I certainly believe that everything the church need, God has provided it in the assembly of Christ. God warns his people about deception and false prophets that will come in the name of Jesus (Matthew 24:4–5), and the church must be able to tell the difference between false prophets and the true prophets of God. Not only false prophets are a concern but also deceptive spirits of "false ministers and teachers" (2 Corinthians 11:3–4; 2 Peter 2:2–3), so God has given some of his children the *spiritual gifts of discern-*

ing between spirits. All spiritual gifts are activated by faith, the Holy Spirit, and the love of Christ Jesus and his children.

The *spiritual gift of speaking in tongues* or the *interpretation of tongues* is another one of God's spiritual gifts he has given to some of his children. This is one of the spiritual gifts that many do not understand and are very seldom used. But what God has given his children is for the building up of his kingdom and edification of his name. In 1 Corinthians 14:27–28, it tells us that "if anyone speaks in a tongue, two—or at the most three—should speak one at a time, and someone must interpret. If there is no interpreter, the speaker should keep quiet in the church and speak to himself and God." Being able to speak in tongues is a spiritual gift from the Lord whereas the speaker is uttering mysteries with his spirit directly to God and without others knowing the conversation except the interpreter. "He who speaks in tongues edifies himself, but he who prophesies edifies the church" (1 Corinthians 14:4).

Now being aware of the different spiritual gifts God has given to his children, one must know that God had also appointed positions in the church such as *apostles*. When Jesus started his ministry, he chose twelve men known as the twelve apostles (Matthew 10:2). The apostles were the first to be chosen by Jesus, and their roles were to equip the saints for service and to edify the body of the church. There was also an *evangelist* who carried the Good News about Jesus Christ. The spreading of the Gospel is their main focus. In Matthew 28:19–20, it states, "Therefore go and make disciples of all nations, baptizing them in the name of the Father, and of the Son, and of the Holy Spirit, and teaching them to obey everything I have commanded you. And surely I am with you always, to the very end of the age." In modern-day times, evangelists are doing the work of the Lord all over the world, and all Christians can take a part in spreading the Good News of Jesus Christ.

"True Ministry Is Using the Principles of God with your Spiritual Gift/s."

Now that we have discussed the different kinds of spiritual gifts, ask yourself: has God given me the Spirit's gift of prophesy, serving, preaching, teaching, encouraging, contributing to the needs of others, leadership, showing mercy, gift of wisdom, knowledge, faith, healing, miraculous powers, discerning between spirits, speaking in tongues, interpretation of tongues, apostles, prophets, evangelist, or some other form of service such as singing in the choir? If you do not know, ask God to allow his Holy Spirit to reveal it to you. In John 16:13–14, it states, "But when the Spirit of truth comes, he will guide you into all truth. He will not speak on his own; he will speak only what he hears, and he will tell you what is yet to come. He will bring glory to me by taking from what is mine and making it known to you."

How to Use Your Spiritual Gift/s God's Way and Reap a Harvest in Your Ministry

*Key Principles—Praying, Love, Compassion, Forgiveness, Faith, and the Holy Spirit to Guide You into Action

Spiritual gifts are blessings from the Lord, which will reap a harvest when used in the right way for the building of the kingdom of the God. The Lord knew the church was going to need instructions, wisdom, knowledge, and understanding, so he sent his Son Jesus Christ (the Word) into the world not only to save the world but also to represent all his Heavenly Father's principles. John 1:1–2 states, "In the beginning was the Word, and the Word was with God, and the Word was God. He was with God in the beginning." Now faith comes by hearing the Word of God.

Praying is an action word…and must be done on a continuous basis (1 Thessalonians 5:17). There will be times in our ministry when we will have to lean on our Heavenly Father for help, strength, assurance, guidance, and for many other situations that may arise while being a ministry leader or being a member of a ministry. Philippians 4:6 states, " Do not be anxious about anything, but in everything by prayer and petition with thanksgiving present your request to God," and Mark 11:24 also states, "Therefore I tell you, whatever you ask for in prayer, believe that you have received it and it will be yours." God wants his ministries to succeed in the church, and he will provide everything for us to make it happen, but one must have a prayer line open to God to his guidance.

Love is an action word…In order to bring about a change, one must have the love of God for God and people. Whether one is working in the church or in the community; the love of God that is within God's children must flow outwardly into the lives of others. All ministries must be exercised in love. The passage in 1 Corinthians 13:1–3 says it best, "If I speak in the tongues of men and of angels, but have not love, I am only a resounding gong or a clanging cymbal. If I have the gift of prophecy and can fathom all mysteries and all knowledge, and if I have a faith than can move mountains, but have not love, I am nothing. If I give all I possess to the poor and surrender my body to the flames, but have not love, I gain nothing." So in everything one does, it must be done in the love of Jesus and our neighbor. Matthew 22:37–40 states, "Love the Lord your God with all your heart and with all your soul and with all your mind. This is the first and greatest commandment. And the second is like it: Love your neighbor as yourself. All the Law and the Prophets hang on these two commandments." All spiritual gifts must be exercised in love, which will bring about a harvest in the ministries of God.

Forgiveness is an action word…There are going to be times in your ministry when forgiving one another must be done. Ephesians 4:32 states "Be kind and compassionate to one another, forgiving each other, just as in Christ God forgave you". Matthew 6:15 states "But if you do not forgive men their sins, your Father will not forgive your sins." Sometimes this action seems hard to do but we must remember Matthew 19:26 which states, "With man this is impossible, but with God all things are possible. So, don't be afraid to cry out to God for help when needed."

Compassion is an action word…In order to bring about a change, one must also have a compassion for what one is doing and compassion for others who are in need and suffering through life's struggles and hardship. The children of God must show compassion in the form of love, kindness, and mercy toward the less fortunate. This form of compassion will bring hope in the lives of others when they see the love of Jesus being poured out into their lives. Matthew 14:14 states, "When Jesus landed and saw a large crowd, he had compassion on them and healed the sick." Also, Matthew 15:32 says, "I have compassion for these people: they have already been with me three days and have nothing to eat. I do not want to send them away hungry, or they may collapse on the way." Another Bible verse that speaks of compassion is in Luke 7:13, which states, "When the Lord saw her, his heart went out to her and he said, 'Don't cry.'" So compassion is necessary and should be exercised in the work of the Lord.

Faith is an action word… Hebrews 11:1 states, "Faith is the things hope for, and the evidence of things not seen." There are going to be situations when the church is going to have to activate their faith in order to receive and deliver the blessings of the Lord Jesus Christ to others. The Word says in Hebrews 11:6, "And without faith it is impossible to please God, because anyone who comes to him must believe that he exists and that he rewards those who earnestly seek him." There are many occasions in the Bible where heroes of faith such as Noah, Abraham, Isaac, Jacob, Joseph, Moses, Joshua, Rahab, and many more exercised their faith in God in order to bring about a blessing to the people of God. In modern-day history, people such as Mother Teresa, Dr. Martin Luther King Jr., James Robison, Joyce Myers, Bill Gates, Bishop T.D. Jakes, Oprah Winfrey, Barack Obama, and many others showed their faith in God to bring about changes in the world. God is requiring us to do the same.

The *Holy Spirit* dwells within the believers of Christ Jesus. When Jesus was getting ready to return to his Heavenly Father, he told his disciples that he was going to send the Holy Spirit to them. John 14:26 states, "But the Counselor, the Holy Spirit, whom the Father will send in my name, will teach you all things and will remind you of everything I have said to you." So Christians must allow the Holy Spirit, who has been sent by our omnipotent, omniscient, and omnipresent God, to be their guide while using their spiritual gifts and key principles. In 1 Corinthians 12:4–7, it states, "There are different kinds of gifts, but the same Spirit. There are different kinds of working, but the same God works all of them in all men. Now to each one the manifestation of the Spirit is given for the common good." The church of God is full of spiritual gifts that are indwelled within the believers for the purpose of uplifting the assembly and glorifying our Heavenly Father. Christians who allow the Holy Spirit to guide them into action, along with the love of Jesus and their neighbors, will see the blessings come through in their ministry. Jesus has revealed to me on occasions his divineness via the Holy Spirit and allowed his divine Word to come alive in my life. While writing this book, Jesus revealed to me that he is certainly human and divine through a "*divine image.*" In a miraculous way the face of Jesus appeared in human form. "In the beginning was the Word, and the Word was with God, and the Word was God" (John1:1). "The Word became flesh and made his dwelling among us. We have seen his glory, the glory of the one and only, who came from the Father, full of grace and truth" (John 1:14). He is the image of the invisible God, the firstborn over all creation. For by him all things were created: things in heaven and on earth, visible and invisible, whether throngs or powers or rulers or authorities, all things were created by him. He is before all things, and in him all things hold together. And he is the head of the body, the church; he is the beginning and the firstborn from among the dead, so that in everything he might have the supremacy (1 Colossians 1:15-18).

How to Sustain Your Ministry

"Making God Your Focus"

When the ministries of God are blessed, they thrive, and sustaining one's ministry becomes the ultimate goal of the Christian leaders. The question is how do Christians continue to have successful ministries within the church? Well, the first and far most focus is God and allowing him to be the center of your ministry. Matthew 6:33 states, "But seek first his kingdom and his righteousness, and all these things will be given to you as well." Secondly, Christians must always maintain a prayer line open to God. Colossians 4:2 states, "Devote yourselves to prayer, being watchful and thankful," and therefore I tell you, whatever you ask for in prayer, believe that you have received it, and it will be yours (Mark 11:24). Thirdly, Christians must always keep their eyes on Jesus as he continues to bless their ministries. Fourth, Christians must continue to listen to the Word of God as he instructs them along the way. Luke 11:28 states, "He replied, 'Blessed rather are those who hear the word of God and obey it.'" Also Christians should continue to keep their hearts and minds on Jesus and block/cancel out anything that is contrary to his purpose.

Philippians 4:8–9 states, "Finally, brothers, whatever is true, whatever is noble, whatever is right, whatever is pure, whatever is lovely, whatever is admirable- if anything is excellent or praiseworthy-think about such things, Whatever you have learned or received or heard from me, or seen in me-put it into practice. And the God of peace will be with you." And the last and foremost, Christians must always operate in the spirit of love. Mark 12:30–31 states, "Love your God with all your heart and with all your soul and with all your mind and with all your strength, the second is this: Love your neighbor as yourself." There is no commandment greater than these." So the package is Christians must pray and guard their eyes, ears, mind, and heart from being infiltrated with negative forces that are coming from outside of the will of God. Then always look to the hills where all your help comes from because in Psalms 121:1–2, it is stated, "I lift up my eyes to the hills—where does my help come from? My help comes from the Lord, the "maker of heaven and earth." And last, again, always operate your ministry in the spirit of love.

A Blessed Ministry Brings Forth Growth in the Church

"Lead in the Ways of God and become a Magnet"

When the people of God are about the will of God, good things began to happen. Ministries in the church began to thrive and grow. Thriving ministries are a blessing not only to the church but also to the community. That's what kingdom building for the Lord is all about. It's pointing people to Christ through the God-given spiritual gifts that are indwelled within the believers of Jesus Christ for his purpose and glory. During the ministries of Jesus, he always drew people to him. Matthew 4:25 says, "Large crowds from Galilee, the Decapolis, Jerusalem, Judea, and the region across the Jordan followed him." When Jesus came down from the mountain, large crowds followed him (Matthew 8:1), so Jesus went with him. A large crowd followed and pressed around him (Mark 5:24). When Jesus heard this, he was amazed at him, and turning to the crowd following him, he said, "I tell you I have not found such great faith even in Israel." Then the men who had been sent returned to the house and found the servant well (Luke 6:9–10). When the children of God exercise their faith and operate their ministries according to the Word, love, and compassion of God, the blessings of the Lord will shower down upon the church, allowing it to grow according to his will. All things are possible with God. Hallelujah!

Thanking God in All Things

"To God Be The Glory"

Thanking God in all things carries so much meaning. The scripture that is so dear to me will sum up the reason why all Christians shall always glorify the Lord and give him thanks in everything. The passage in 1 Chronicles 16:34 tells us to "give thanks to the Lord, for he is good; for his love endures forever!" The first part of that scripture, "Give thanks to the Lord, for he is good," is a statement that should cause one to pause, take a deep breath, sigh…and look around and see all the good things in our lives and in the world, which God has blessed us with. While living in a world that is filled with trials and tribulations, we are so quick to forget to just think about the goodness of God.

John 16:33 states, "I have told you these things, so that in me you may have peace. In this world you will have trouble, but take heart! I have overcome the world." So no matter what may be troubling to you, continue to give thanks to our Heavenly Father because certainly he is so good to be praised. "Be joyful always; pray continually; give thanks in all circumstances, for this is God's will for you in Christ Jesus" (1 Thessalonians 5:16–18). The second part of the scripture, "For his love endures forever," is like a covenant that God has made to his children that will never be broken…" For I am convinced that neither death nor life, neither angels nor demons, neither the present nor the future, nor depth, nor anything else in all creation will be able to separate us from the love of God that is in Christ Jesus our Lord" (Romans 8:38–39). Just knowing that the love of Jesus will never end is very serene…and that's why Christians who are the helping hands of God, the eyes of God, the listening ears of God, the traveling feet of God, and the voice of God should always remember while serving in their ministry to give thanks to the Lord, for he is good and his love endures forever and ever and ever!

Conclusion

Having a productive ministry is very important to the welfare of the Church and to the community in which we serve, near and abroad. God never intended for his Church (the believers in Christ) to be stagnated or non-productive when it comes to serving God and pointing people to Christ Jesus. God has given everyone Spiritual gift/s for the upbuilding of his kingdom and for the edification of his name. Growing your ministry God's way will always bring about love, peace, happiness, and thriving ministries that will give evident that Jesus Christ who is *human and divine* is alive and well, and sitting on the right-hand side of his Father in Heaven, waiting for us to cry out to Him for help when needed to do his will.

About the Author

Hi, my name is Gertrude Joanne Pollard-Watts, and I have been studying the Word of God for many years. I am grateful for having the opportunity to teach the adult Sunday school class for fourteen years and will always love serving the Lord in that spiritual gift. I gave my life to God at an early age and have ever since found myself wanting to learn about him more and more throughout the years. I attended Grand Canyon University (a wonderful college to attend with campus and online programs) and earned a Bachelor of Arts degree in Christian Studies as well as a Master's Degree in Christian Studies with an emphasis in Pastoral Ministry. After a year passed, once again, I found myself enrolling again in college to earn a Doctor of Education (Ed. D.) degree in Organizational Leadership with an emphasis in Christian Ministry. Nearly a year into the program and with a revelation from God through a sermon preached by Rev. Dr. Charles E. Goodman, Jr. (Tabernacle Baptist Church-West, Evans, GA), made me realize I was searching for something which God had already given and placed inside of me...the gift of being a Spiritual writer/author who writes Christian faith-based and inspirational books for his glory. The sermon came from Genesis 25:29-34...Certainly I didn't want to give up the blessings of the Lord by reaching for something else. Even though I knew that education is very important and should be pursued, I also knew that recognizing the voice of God and his guidance and obeying it must be done. I began to change focus and dismissed myself from the program and started completing *this* book which was laid aside. Visiting Tabernacle Baptist Church-West was the beginning of a changed life for me, and I thank God for his Word that was brought forth in my life.

Theology has always been my passion. Not only do I love learning about God, but I also love to share what I have learned and has been revealed to me with others. Being a teacher of the Word of God and an author are not the only thing God has for me to do while on earth, but for now…I am going to enjoy spreading the Good News about Jesus Christ through those blessings.

~I pray may God continue to bless you and your ministry always~

www.ingramcontent.com/pod-product-compliance
Lightning Source LLC
Chambersburg PA
CBHW021413290426
44108CB00010B/517